Wait a Minute!

thirty devotions inspired
by life's breath-catching
moments

MARY K. SELZER

ISBN-13: 9781518693106

TABLE OF CONTENTS

dedication

to my parents George and Mary Wartian who raised their four children in the nurture and admonition of the Lord and taught us to love God's word

INTRODUCTION

S omeone has said that in a 75-year life span the average person will spend 23 years sleeping, 19 years working, nine years playing, six years traveling, six years eating, four years being sick, two years getting dressed and one year in church. A lot can happen in a lifetime, and sometimes life seems to move at lightning speed. Before we know it, we're lamenting, "Where did the time go?"

In our lifetimes we will experience millions of minutes. If we stop long enough, we can find that each moment is an experience. Experiences turn into lessons, and lessons become legacies.

Wait A Minute is intended to encourage you to slow down and capture significance from life's breath-catching moments. I hope you will emerge at the end of this book aware of those specific times in your own life where learning was obvious but the lesson was missed. When you do, just catch your breath and take a second look. You'll find what you missed the first time.

Take a moment to wait a minute.

Mary

A LESSON FROM THE ORANGE PEEL

 "Each one should use whatever gift he has received to serve others." 1 Peter 4:10

Several years ago *Reader's Digest* published an article written by a frustrated housewife. Her day was the worst possible, including a sick dog, a sink full of dishes and a broken clothes dryer. With mounds of laundry waiting to be done, she draped the freshly-laundered clothes throughout the family room.

Shortly after arranging her husband's various clothing items across the furniture, the doorbell rang. There, unannounced, stood her high school boyfriend and his perfectly stunning blond wife. She opened the door and led them through the family room with the laundry-covered couch, clumsily explaining about the broken dryer. As she tried to apologize and fix coffee, she spotted a "long, shriveled, dusty orange peel" curled up in the middle of the floor as if it had been there for weeks. The boyfriend and his wife watched as the frustrated housewife tried to slide it to one side with her foot. It stuck. She had to peel it off like adhesive tape.

The rest of the visit was a blur to her, and she was only too happy when the couple departed.

She cried as she related the story to her husband later that day. His words were slightly soothing, to say the least: "Well, honey, just think of how good you made them feel today. His wife knows you're no threat and he's glad he never married you. Don't think of *your* ego; think what you're doing for *their* marriage."[1]

When was the last time you made someone else feel good at your own expense? No matter how hard we try, it seems to go against our human nature, doesn't it? But, we are called to serve; and if we are sincerely serving, the other person(s) will be more gratified than we are. That's exactly what Jesus modeled. Jesus never did anything for his own benefit.

Who was satisfied after the he served bread and fish to the 5,000 after three straight days of ministry? When the blind stopped him in his tracks as they called out for healing, who received and who gave? Whose grief was relieved when Lazarus was raised from the dead? When he spent over three years with twelve unlearned men, who benefited the most? When he laid down his life for mankind, who felt better?

Everything Jesus did was for someone else's benefit. "The Son of man did not come to be served, but to serve" (Matthew 20:28).

Imagine a world where everyone puts everyone else first. Since that might be close to impossible, think what would happen in a *church* if we were devoted to making the other members feel good at our own expense?

Maybe we need to show a little more orange peel and a little less self.

---

[1] From an article by Robin Worthington (*Reader's Digest*, October, 1973) p. 77

Prayer

Jesus, you are the perfect model of a servant. Please forgive me for those selfish moments when I put my needs above the needs of others. Give me grace to allow myself to be vulnerable, and help me devote myself for the benefit of others. Amen

TABLE TALK

 "Then those who feared the Lord talked with each other, and the Lord listened and heard. A scroll of remembrance was written in his presence concerning those who feared the Lord and honored his name." Malachi 3:16

An old adage says, *"Eavesdroppers seldom hear anything good of themselves."* Everyone knows that eavesdropping is not polite, and those who do it certainly don't admit it. Here's the ironic truth about God—He eavesdrops. And he makes it known that he does.

The prophet Malachi was correcting the Israelites for numerous infractions, including defiled sacrifices (1:10), faulty leadership (2:1), and failure to give God what was rightfully his (3:8-9). But the entire nation wasn't guilty. There was a remnant of God-fearers who expressed their concern about the condition of their country. Maybe they sat at the city gates and quietly conversed. Or perhaps they chatted over dinner, breaking bread while they broke down their issues of unease.

Wherever they were, we know this—those individuals who talked amongst themselves were not praying. They were simply voicing their concern about the state of the nation. Something about what they said and how they said it captured God's attention. Not only did he listen. He recorded who they were, what they said and the fact that they were among "those who feared the Lord."

People who fear God carry a healthy respect and a sacred acknowledgement that he is the ultimate Authority and his decisions are 100% just and fair. God-fearers know there are consequences for disobedience, and they choose to follow God, not to avoid those consequences, but because they understand the value of pleasing God through obedience. True God-fearers are God-pleasers. No wonder they had God's attention!

Do you realize what this verse can do for our faith? It can completely eradicate the lie that we don't have enough faith for God to respond. Any argument that God has lifted his hand from the church or our nation is blown out of the water. And the spiritual toil of trying to be good enough for God to pay attention to our feeble prayers will dissipate.

Next time you're at Starbucks holding a serious conversation with other God-fearing friends, remember that he doesn't just hear our prayers. He heeds our conversations. Who knows? He may also enjoy the aroma of coffee.

Prayer

Lord, I can't thank you enough that even when I'm not directing my conversation to you, you are interested enough to pay attention and record what I say. When I converse with other God-fearing people, check us if our words become too wearisome; and correct us if our conversations stimulate more fear over our concerns than we have toward you. You are welcome to join us for coffee any time we meet. Amen

LILIES AND BIRDS

"Do not worry about your life, what you will eat or drink; or about your body, what you will wear. Look at the birds of the air; they do not sow or reap or store away in barns, and yet your heavenly Father feeds them. Are you not much more valuable than they? See how the lilies of the field grow. They do not labor or spin. Yet I tell you that not even Solomon in all his splendor was dressed like one of these. If that is how God clothes the grass of the field, will he not much more clothe you?" Matthew 6:25-30

Eugene and Phyllis Grams served as missionaries to South Africa for close to fifty years, supported by churches and friends. Our church happened to be Phyllis' home church and, when they came to the States on furlough, they often ministered to our congregation. One time Eugene shared how early in their ministry donations had slowed down to almost nothing. They were in desperate need of finances. Every day he would walk to the mailbox, hoping someone had sent them the much-needed money. Each time he was disappointed. Before long their family had nothing more to eat than beets.

On his daily trips to the mailbox he noticed a scrap of paper stuck by the fence in their yard. "I need to pick that up," he thought to himself as he continued toward the mailbox. After several days of disappointment and beets, he meandered along the fence to pick up the scrap paper. To his shock it was an envelope from our church addressed simply "Eugene Grams, South Africa." Inside was a generous check. The famine was over. "If only I had picked up that scrap paper earlier," he lamented. "Then we wouldn't have had to eat beets three times a day."

At the beginning of Jesus' ministry with his disciples, he instructed them not to worry. "Your heavenly Father knows [what] you need." It was important training for his inexperienced followers. God taught Eugene and Phyllis, as new missionaries, the same thing: He will provide—and he'll pleasantly surprise them in the process. Lessons learned early are long remembered and soon become the catalyst for increased faith.

Next time you're worried about your lack of provision, remember this—if God can direct a partially-addressed envelope to one particular man in a country measuring over 471,000 square miles, he can certainly deliver to your corner of the world.

Prayer
Father, thank you for your boundless provisions. When worry creeps in, please remind me of your care for the smallest of creatures. Help me learn faith lessons quickly so my trust in you grows and I can believe you for the miraculous. Amen

ACTIVE WAITING

 "Wait for the Lord; be strong and take heart and wait for the Lord." Psalm 27:14

T he newbie author was becoming very impatient as he waited to hear from the publisher about his manuscript. He texted a friend who had published several books and asked, "What do I do while I'm waiting to hear if my manuscript has been accepted?" The response was brief: "Keep writing."

Waiting can seem like a waste of time. But if we don't learn to wait, we could be wasting even more time. Like a friend I have who loathes red lights because they're a "waste of time" (her words). Instead of waiting for the light to turn green, she maneuvers her vehicle through side streets until she finds her way back to the main road. "As long as I'm moving, I'm making progress," she says defensively. I've tried to reason with her that if she would wait thirty more seconds, the light would turn green and she could continue on her way without taking the more circuitous route. "Doing nothing is fruitless," she declared. "I can't sit that long."

Waiting is not the same as being idle. According to the Psalmist, we are to practice *active waiting*. "Wait for the Lord;

be strong and **take heart**." Active waiting builds our strength because we anticipate what God has next for us. At the same time, our confidence increases so we will be ready to step in when he gives the signal.

A friend spent almost two years waiting for a certain transition to be completed so he could move into a new ministry position. He struggled with feelings of depression and uselessness. Another minister urged him to take advantage of the down time, encouraging him to study and prepare sermons as if he were stepping into the pulpit the following Sunday. Throughout the process, my friend became stronger spiritually and emotionally and, when the Lord opened a door of ministry, he was ready to step through it with confidence. He had learned the secret of active waiting.

Isaiah's words are bolstering: "[The Lord] gives strength to the weary and increases the power of the weak. Even youths grow tired and weary and young men stumble and fall; but those who wait on the Lord will renew their strength. They will soar on wings like eagles; they will run and not grow weary, they will walk and not be faint" (Isaiah 40:29-31).

Now I can't wait to fly!

Prayer
Lord, teach me the value of active waiting. Pull me back when impatience pushes me ahead of you. Urge me on when idleness causes me to lag. As I wait, help me build muscle so I will be strong enough for my next assignment, and increase my confidence so I can move forward without fear. Amen

NAMING GOD

 "Abraham called that place The Lord Will Provide. And to this day it is said, 'On the mountain of the Lord it will be provided'." Genesis 22:14

"I've given God a new name!" a woman excitedly announced in our Bible study group. "I now call him 'The God of the Detroit Freeways.' I've always been afraid to drive on the expressway and the other day God gave me courage and peace to reach my destination! Now I'm not afraid anymore."

Some members of the class looked at each other a little puzzled. One woman asked, "Can we do that? Can we actually give God a new name?" According to the Bible, yes we can! In fact, it may be one of the highest forms of worship to God because giving him a new name means our relationship with him has become more intimate. Consider these examples in scripture:

1. When God told Abraham to sacrifice his son Isaac as a test of his faith and trust in God, an angel stopped him just as Abraham was ready to plunge the knife

into Isaac's chest. Abraham looked up and saw a ram caught in a thicket. He sacrificed the ram as a burnt offering instead of his son (see Genesis 22:1-14). Then Abraham called God a name he had never before been called: *The Lord Will Provide.*

2. In Exodus 17 we read of the battle between the Israelites and the Amalekites. During the course of the conflict, Moses stood with the staff of God raised high, like a banner. As long as the "banner" waved, the Israelites were winning, but when Moses' hands became weary and he lowered them, the Amalekites were winning. Two men—Aaron and Hur—stood on either side of Moses and held his hands up in an attempt to keep the banner high. Following the Israelites' victory, Moses gave God a new name: *The Lord is my Banner.*

3. An angel appeared to Gideon and told him he would lead the Israelites to victory against the Midianites. As an act of honor, Gideon prepared a meal for the angel who touched the food with the tip of his staff, causing fire to consume the meat and bread. Gideon panicked because he realized he had seen the Lord and thought he would die (see Exodus 33:20). The angel assured him, "Peace! Do not be afraid. You are not going to die" (see Judges 6:11-24). Gideon built an altar and, because of the unforgettable encounter with the Lord, he named him *The Lord is Peace.*

Abraham, Moses and Gideon gave God names *he had never before been called!* It was their testimony of God's ability to provide, protect and keep his promise.

What's your testimony? Now, give God a new name.

Prayer

Lord, please keep me aware of everything you do for me—whether great or small. Help me be more diligent in acknowledging you and testifying of your greatness. Then when I call you by a new name, please accept it as my sincere act of worship. Amen

SHORT MEMORY

 "One thing I do: Forgetting those things which are behind and straining toward what is ahead, I press on toward the goal to win the prize for which God has called me heavenward in Christ Jesus." Philippians 3:13-14

The phone call was not pleasant. A disgruntled choir member decided to air her grief over not being selected as the main soloist. Her allegations were so unbelievable that I wrote them down word for word—in shorthand. After the thirty-minute diatribe, I lamely apologized and hung up the phone. "Unbelievable," I muttered to myself as I reviewed the notes. Then I carefully tucked the paper next to the phone for safekeeping. Every time the phone rang, I saw the notes and shook my head in disbelief.

"Get rid of those notes," the Lord challenged me one day. "You don't need to remember that conversation."

"But, Lord," I argued, "It's proof to me that she was wrong and I was right."

"If you keep those notes," he said, "You will build up bitterness in your heart and I will not be able to bless you."

I desperately wanted to obey, but I wasn't sure I could let it go. So, I partially obeyed. Before tossing the notes, I committed them to memory—just in case.

God dealt with me again to release the situation. "Ask me to help you forget what she said to you," he offered. It was difficult for me to let go because I needed that information so I would have something to hold against her. However, my spiritual growth was at stake and it just wasn't worth jeopardizing my relationship with the Lord by holding on to such an unpleasant memory. So, I boldly asked God to wipe from my mind the details of the conversation.

And he did—almost immediately! To this day I can recall only that she falsely accused me. The details of the conversation are gone. It was God's way of protecting my heart from bitterness that would have become an unnecessary weight. It's extremely difficult to run a race with extra baggage, isn't it?

The apostle Paul uses three action verbs in Philippians 3:13-14 that can change how we run life's race: Forget, strain and press. *Forgetting* is an intentional action on our part to push away from anything (including unpleasant or hurtful memories) that might keep our attention on the past. *Straining* means we deliberately force ourselves to move and look forward as we *press* (persevere) toward the Lord.

How can we do this? By keeping our minds clear of clutter and keeping our running shoes on at all times.

Prayer

Lord, please give me a long memory of you and your blessings. Give me a short memory of hurtful or painful circumstances. Forgive me for holding on to unhealthy thoughts because they really do weigh me down. Help me run the race with a pure heart and a clear conscience. Increase my speed and help me keep my eyes on you. Thank you in advance. Amen

STORM WATCHERS

 "He who dwells in the shelter of the Most High will rest in the shadow of the Almighty. I will say of the Lord, 'He is my refuge and my fortress, my God, in whom I trust.' If you make the Most High your dwelling—even the Lord, who is my refuge—then no harm will befall you, no disaster will come near your tent." Psalm 91:1-2, 9-10

We used to live in a home with a windowed back porch that ran the length of the house. It was a great play area for our kids. When the weather was warm, we opened the windows and enjoyed a wonderful breeze. Our kids' favorite thing, though, was to watch storms from the porch—with mom and dad present, of course. All of us would sit encompassed within the safety of the windowed fortress and watch the torrents of rain run down the windows while we remained safe and dry. That is until the raging winds or tornado siren drove us into the security of the house. Thank God we had a back-up plan!

Weather-related storms are fascinating to watch—from a safe distance, that is. Programs on the Discovery Channel or movies like *Twister* allow us to get close enough to danger without fear of harm because we are observing within the safety of our own homes. Push the power button on the remote and the storm disappears.

Wouldn't it be wonderful if life's storms could be treated the same way? We may not have an "on/off" button to control the storms, but we do have a choice where and how we observe. Hands down, the safest place to be during a storm is in the most secure shelter. That's why God said if we "dwell" (abide, remain) within His shelter, we will "rest" (sleep, be at peace) in His shadow. He wants us in the house, not on the back porch.

Looking back, I can see how I have treated God as my "back-up" plan instead of my first go-to. I have spent too much time on the back porch analyzing, fretting and talking to others about my storms. The problem is I emerge knowing more about the storm and what caused it than I do the Protector in the midst of the storm. Isn't learning something new about God worth going through a storm?

Our daughters are now married with families of their own. One of them lives in a part of the country that is notorious for tornadoes. When the sirens sound, she and her husband calmly lead their children to the basement where they have prepared a little play area for storm emergencies. They read books and play games while mom and dad wait for the all-clear signal. The children are unaware of potential danger because they remain in the presence of their parents who protect them from harm by leading them to the most secure place. The children are too young and innocent to even know what a back-up plan is. But, they are trusting enough to know that mom and dad would never lead them into harm's way.

Are you facing a storm? Learn something, go to sleep and wake up refreshed.

Prayer

Father, you have thought of everything, including preparing a safe place in the midst of life's storms. Please help me reside in your presence and not treat you as a back-up plan. I want to know more about you than I know about the storms. May every challenge I face be a learning experience about you, and may I emerge rested and refreshed. Amen

STUCK AT THE BOTTOM OF A BOX

"For this is what the Lord says . . .without money you will be redeemed." Isaiah 52:3

"Better to sell it for a quarter than keep it for nothing." This was the motto purported by the coordinator of our church rummage sale. So, when I found a small saucer hidden at the bottom of a box of donated items, I ignored its appearance and dutifully stuck it with a twenty-five cent label. The plate soon found itself on a folding table holding numerous other cheap things.

Fortunately, another worker with a keener eye than mine saw possible value in the plate. She took it to an antique dealer who gasped when she saw the beautiful flower painted in the center of the dish. "Why this is an original Majolica!" she exclaimed, ripping off the twenty-five cent sticker. "This plate is worth at least $35!" And she bought it. How unfortunate that such a beautiful, valuable plate would end up relegated to the bottom of a box of devalued stuff.

The Lord reminded me of another time when I failed to recognize true value. Only this time it involved a person, not a plate. A woman attended our church for a short time. Her outward appearance was not attractive and her hygiene was—well—in need of serious attention. Her hair was stringy and her clothes ill-fitting. A couple of times I gave her a ride home and, even though it was wintertime, I kept my window down to avoid the unpleasant odor coming from the passenger's side. The day she told us she was moving and would have to find a closer church, I secretly rejoiced—much to my shame.

Several months later, she called to tell me a woman at her new church was taking her for a complete make-over, including new clothes and a fresh hairstyle. "Wow," I said, suppressing a little tinge of guilt. "That's wonderful. What's the occasion?"

"No special occasion," she responded. "The woman said she saw value in me and wanted to help me look good."

Obviously, I had a serious flaw in my vision. I couldn't recognize beauty when it stared me in the face, and I couldn't see potential when it sat next to me in my car! Thank God He can spot both beauty and potential, whether He's looking at an individual—or an entire nation, like Israel.

No matter how rebellious the Israelites were, God never lost hope in them. He always recognized their true value and often spoke through the prophets to underscore that truth. In their original form, the Israelites were God's chosen people, highly favored and set apart from all others. However, they compromised their covenant with the Lord and, after resisting numerous opportunities to repent, ended up in Babylonian captivity for seventy years.

In the midst of their bondage, God looked at the bottom of the box and saw more than a discarded nation. Despite the Israelites' defects, the Lord acknowledged their true worth and tagged them with a promise to redeem them without money (a prophetic word about Jesus who paid the ultimate price by giving his own life). They didn't deserve it, but God couldn't help himself. He's drawn to devalued throw-aways because he knows the original value.

Sometimes we may feel like we're stuck at the bottom of a box—forgotten and worthless. How did we get there? Whether someone else did it to us, or whether we did it to ourselves, it's not too late to be rescued. The Master is dying to retrieve us and restore our natural beauty. If we let him, he'll remove the old labels and mark us as his originals. We may not deserve it, but he just can't help himself.

Are you ready to get out of the box?

Prayer

Lord, thank you for seeing enough value in my life to redeem me with yours. I give you permission to pull me from the bottom of the box so I can fulfill your purpose for my life. Help me treat others with the same kindness you have shown me so I can help them fulfill their purpose as well.

ENTERTAINING ANGELS

 "Do not forget to entertain strangers, for by so doing some people have entertained angels without knowing it. Remember those in prison as if you were their fellow prisoners, and those who are mistreated as if you yourselves were suffering." Hebrews 13:2

"Whatever you did for one of the least of these brothers of mine, you did for me." Matthew 25:40

I remember a story my mother told me. It happened in the early 1940's. My parents were new believers. My father had just started his own business and money was tight. One cold, blustery day while he was at work, the doorbell rang at the house. When my mother went to the door, she found a stranger shivering from the cold. "Lady," he began, "I'm so hungry and it's so cold out here. I need food for my family. Could you please help me out?"

Without giving it a second thought, she invited him in and offered to make him a hot lunch. He devoured the soup and sandwich and said over and over, "This is so good. Thank you. Thank you so much."

As he was preparing to leave, she gave him a couple bags of food for his family. Again he thanked her profusely and headed for the front door. By the time she got to the door to tell him good-bye, he was gone. And there were no footprints in the snow.

Whenever my mother told me this story—numerous times—she would look at me wide-eyed and say, "I think I fed an angel and didn't know it."

I love this story. I've told it to my daughters—numerous times—and can't wait to tell it to my grandchildren when they're old enough to understand. God does send angels on assignment and always with a specific purpose to fulfill.

Angels appeared to Abraham and Sarah (Genesis 18:2-22), Lot (Genesis 19:1-2), Manoah and his wife (Judges 13:2-14), and Gideon (Judges 6:11-20). In each situation, the angels delivered messages of hope, encouragement or warning. The people recognized them as messengers from the Lord and offered warm hospitality.

If angels who appeared in Bible times had a specific purpose, what assignment do angels have who might appear in modern times—such as the case of the apparent angel who showed up at my mother's door? He had no message. He was just hungry. Is it possible that God uses angels in order to test our level of hospitality to strangers? According to Matthew 25:34-40, it's a *strong* possibility, since people will be judged by their attentiveness to the hungry, needy, imprisoned and sick.

How do the angels feel about their awkward assignments to appear as needy humans? In Psalm 103:20-21 we learn that obedience prevails. "Praise the Lord, you his angels, you mighty ones who do his bidding, who obey his word. Praise the Lord, all his heavenly hosts, you his servants who do his will."

Maybe if we were more obedient to the opportunities that come our way, it would be less awkward for us to associate with people of lower position. We may not be angels, but God wants to send us on awkward assignments. Will we pass the test, or will he have to send someone else?

Prayer

Jesus, I want to be as willing and obedient as the angels who obey your word and do your bidding. Please forgive me for judging the needy. Help me, instead, to be attentive to their needs so you can trust me with future assignments. Amen

STRESS OR DISTRESS?

 "In my distress I called to the Lord; I cried to my God for help. From his temple he heard my voice; my cry came before him, into his ears . . . he parted the heavens and came down." Psalm 18:6, 9

Have you ever wished you could live a stress-free life? The bad news is that if your life is stress-free, you're probably not alive. The good news is that stress can be healthy. It's when we turn stress into *distress* that we bear unnecessary consequences.

Seamstresses know that thread tension is necessary for a sewing machine to function well. The machine is set up to create just the right amount of tension. Too much tension will cause the thread to break. Not enough will render the thread useless because it just flops around and holds nothing together.

God has designed difficult circumstances in life with the perfect amount of stress—just enough to help us develop perseverance so we can build character, but not so much that we break. Stress is part of life. Our response, however, becomes the tipping point that determines if the stress will turn into *distress.*

When David wrote Psalm 18, he was in a situation that neither you nor I have ever faced—he was being pursued by King Saul who wanted to kill him. David's life was a challenge starting with his teenage years. God had Samuel anoint him king of Israel while the current king (Saul) was still on the throne. Then God arranged for David to serve in the king's palace to provide music therapy whenever Saul went into one of his violent rages. On one occasion, Saul went ballistic and threw a spear at David while he was playing his harp. Talk about stress!

To make matters worse, David escaped and hid in a cave where men who were "in distress or in debt or discontented gathered around him, and he became their leader" (1 Samuel 22:1-2). Now David *really* was in a stressful situation because he was surrounded by four hundred dysfunctional people. What was God thinking?

God is more concerned about our *response* to challenging situations than he is about the situation itself because he knows life's trials will strengthen us. Paul said, ". . . we also rejoice in our sufferings, because we know that suffering produces perseverance; perseverance, character; and character, hope. And hope does not disappoint us, because God has poured out his love into our hearts by the Holy Spirit" (Romans 5:3-5).

Scripture indicates David didn't ascend to the throne until the age of thirty (see 2 Samuel 5:4). What happened between the time he was anointed and the time he actually assumed the king's role? God was giving him the heart of a king.

The Psalms are filled with David's laments about his enemies and his often impossible conditions. But when David had opportunity to kill King Saul, he refused to touch the

"Lord's anointed," even though he was urged on by his own men (see 1 Samuel 24:6-7).

For around fifteen years David lived in stress—and sometimes the stress turned to distress. God monitored David carefully and when circumstances became too tense, the Lord became his support (see Psalm 18:18). God was never early—lest David miss the opportunity to build his strength. And he was never late—lest David be crushed from the distress of his situation.

Is your life stressful? Learn to live with the stress and call on the Lord in your *dis*tress. God monitors you and me as closely as he did David. His timing is as perfect as his will.

David ended up becoming what God wanted—a man after his own heart (1 Samuel 13:14). Was it worth the stress? I believe David would say, "Absolutely!"

Prayer

Lord, I'm not asking you to remove stress from my life because I know how vital it is for me to build character as I endure trials. So I am simply asking that you give me the grace to persevere through the storms of life; and when I'm in over my head, please be to me what you were to David—my rock, my fortress and my deliverer. Give me the spirit of David so I can be considered a person after your own heart. Amen

THE SUBTLETY OF JEALOUSY

 Do nothing out of selfish ambition or vain conceit, but in humility consider others better than yourselves. Each of you should look not only to your own interests, but also to the interests of others." Philippians 2:3

Evangelist Dwight L. Moody told the fable of an eagle that was jealous of another that could outfly him. One day he saw a sportsman and said, "I wish you would bring that eagle down." The sportsman replied he would only if he had some feathers to put into his arrow. So the eagle pulled one out of his wing. The arrow was shot, but didn't quite reach the rival eagle because it was flying too high. The envious eagle kept pulling out more feathers until he lost so many he couldn't fly. Then the sportsman turned around and killed him. Moody concluded, *"My friend, if you are jealous, the only man you can hurt is yourself."*

Jealousy isn't hard to camouflage because most people fight the battle with it internally. The Bible, however, is quite clear that it is a sin, no matter where the battle is fought, and it should be avoided at all costs (see Galatians 5:20; Romans 13:13-14).

While envy is the desire to have what someone else has, jealousy is the selfish desire to keep what I have to myself. The cause of jealousy has often been whittled down to insecurity, lack of confidence or low self-esteem. However, it has a more subtle side. Jealousy is often masked in the need that makes us want to be, look or perform better than anyone else. If I can be the person with the unique talent, then I can stand out and be noticed. If no one else can do it, have it or become it, the spotlight and the attention are all mine.

I knew a woman who was very skilled in making a unique and extremely beautiful craft. Her displays always evoked "oohs" and "aahs" from onlookers. When she was asked to teach a class and share with others how to make the craft, she declined. Later she confessed she wanted to guard her talent jealously because it set her apart from everyone else. If others learned what she could do, she would lose her significance.

Paul admonished, "Honor one another above yourselves" (Romans 12:10). In order to do that, we will have to let them fly higher than we can. When we do, the internal struggle with jealousy will cease. Instead, we can enjoy inner peace knowing we inspired someone else. In the end, we will all soar.

Prayer

Jesus, you know my inner struggles and how hard my sinful nature fights to be noticed. Forgive me for not fighting back as hard as I should. Please help me not to do anything out of selfish conceit but instead to consider others better than myself. Thank you for the example you have already set. By your grace I will follow. Amen

A CITY WITHOUT WALLS

 "Like a city whose walls are broken down is a man who lacks self-control." Proverbs 25:28

Solomon sat secure on the throne of Israel while he enjoyed a reign of peace. He had built a beautiful temple where people could worship. The walls around the city were nearly impenetrable. Jerusalem was secure spiritually and physically. It was the best of times.

However, Solomon wasn't as vigilant about protecting his own heart as he was about guarding his kingdom. Although God had cautioned him to remain faithful by keeping his commands, decrees and laws, Solomon married many foreign women who introduced him to idol worship and eventually led his heart astray. Solomon had failed to reinforce the wall around his heart and, in time, he became like the proverbial "city whose walls are broken down."

What does a city with broken walls and a man without self-control have in common? They are both unguarded territories that can be easily invaded. Where there is no fortification or control, anything can enter and exit; and, in time, a person yields control to someone or something that does not belong.

Self-control is an internal quality that affects external actions. Lack of self-control is usually manifested in more ways than one. However, if we can develop discipline in one area, we will find it easier to have restraint in others because we are developing the quality of self-control. Whether we've lost control of our temper, our tongue, our appetite, our morals, our finances or our time, God will help us regain control if we will (1) acknowledge the need and (2) persevere.

The Bible is paradoxical when it speaks of developing self-control. Paul indicates in Galatians 5:23 that it is part of the fruit of the Spirit and grows as naturally as a tree bears fruit. As one teacher said, a tree doesn't bear fruit to *prove* it's a fruit tree. It bears fruit *because* it's a fruit tree.

Peter, however, indicates that the responsibility to develop self-control is up to us. "*Make every effort* to add to your faith goodness; and to goodness, knowledge; and to knowledge, *self-control;* and to self-control, perseverance . . ." (2 Peter 1:5-6).

So, which is it? Natural proliferation or self effort? It's both. God's Spirit works in us to remove anything that might prevent the fruit of the Spirit from fully developing. The more he reveals unprotected areas, the more diligent we must be to fortify ourselves by reading the Word regularly, praying, listening to wise counsel and staying accountable.

One young man who was saved out of a very immoral lifestyle told his mentor he thought God wanted him to return to those with whom he had been immoral and witness to them. His mentor wisely warned that he could be entering a den of temptation that he was not yet strong enough to face. Instead, his mentor advised, he should ask God to send someone else to speak to his former friends about their need for the Lord. Wise counsel.

In Solomon's later years, he spent a lot of time reminiscing about life. Some say he became cynical and pessimistic. His own carelessness resulted in vulnerability that led to regretted choices. However, one man's failure can become another man's fortification. At one point Solomon wrote, "Whoever breaks through a wall may be bitten by a snake" (Ecclesiastes 10:8). Before we're bitten, let's learn from the one who was.

Prayer

Lord, please help me guard my heart and strengthen areas that are weak and vulnerable. I am willing to take responsibility by controlling what is out of control. I realize I need your Spirit to nourish my heart so more fruit will grow on every branch of my life. Amen

DRIVEN OR LED?

 "He leads beside still waters." Psalm 23:2

A young pastor talked excitedly about his new ministry and the plethora of ideas running through his head. *"This ministry is going to succeed,"* he declared, *"because I'm driven to success."*

Driven to success. Those are powerful words. When we are "driven," someone or something else is in control, as if an invisible force pushes from behind toward an unknown destination. We might be moving forward, but we are not necessarily achieving success.

I know when I'm being "driven," because my life suddenly feels overloaded and confusing—almost to the point of panic. People's expectations, impulsive commitments, competition or my own pride at one time or another have pushed me to destinations God never intended. It's difficult to slow down and catch my breath because the force behind me overpowers my ability to pray or think clearly. Life becomes more like an overwhelming tsunami instead of the "still waters" where God leads.

When scripture refers to something being "driven," it is almost always in the context that something needed to be removed or someone was defeated. For example, God "drove out" the enemy from the Promised Land (Joshua 23:9). The Israelites were "driven back" in defeat (Joshua 8:15). The Israelites were "driven" into exile by their enemies (Amos 9:4). The demon-possessed man was "driven" by the demon (Luke 8:29). Jesus "drove out" the evil spirits (Matthew 8:16).

Hirelings who oversee the flocks are drivers. They push from behind with little concern for the sheep because they have no ownership. Jesus warned "The hired hand is not the shepherd who owns the sheep. So when he sees the wolf coming, he abandons the sheep and runs away" (John 10:12). The hireling drives from the back, wielding the rod to push the sheep forward—the same rod a shepherd uses to "comfort" the sheep because of the security it represents (Psalm 23:4).

The hireling may drive the flock from behind, but the Good Shepherd leads his sheep from the front. Sometimes his leadership takes us through difficult storms where we learn to hold on to him and trust. Other times he brings us to quiet places beside still waters where we can relax and refresh. And when our lives get out of control, he "makes us" lie down in green pastures because he knows we need to slow down and rest.

What's driving you? Stop and refocus on the leading Shepherd. You'll find great comfort knowing he will never take you where he has not already walked.

Prayer

Jesus, thank you that you don't drive your sheep. Instead, you gently lead. I love how you slow me down enough to enjoy the still waters. If I ever challenge your judgment and retort, "You can't make me!" <u>please</u> make me lie down in green pastures. And don't let me get up until my steps are in sync with your will. Amen

THE SAFEST WAY TO THE TOP

 "When you are invited, take the lowest place, so that when your host comes, he will say to you, 'Friend, move up to a better place.' Then you will be honored in the presence of all your fellow guests. For everyone who exalts himself will be humbled and he who humbles himself will be exalted." Luke 14:10-11

I once belonged to an organization that offered annual awards for various accomplishments—leadership, innovation, creativity, etc. Members were encouraged to nominate other members who they thought merited the awards and then a select committee made the final decisions. One year a particular woman who thought she deserved to be honored made calls to fellow members asking someone to please nominate her. "I really think I should be nominated because of the years I've served our organization."

Her prideful attitude worked against her because she couldn't find anyone who agreed to make the nomination. Although she was extremely gifted, she sought for recognition but ended up without it. Apparently she wasn't familiar with

Solomon's caution—"Let another praise you, and not your own mouth; someone else and not your own lips" (Proverbs 27:2).

When Jesus gave the instructions in Luke 14 to "take the lowest place," he was addressing guests who were picking places of honor at the dinner table in the house of a prominent Pharisee. Imagine the chaos as people vied for the best spots— close to the popular host, no doubt.

Later Jesus even cautioned the host to guard his motives when giving a party, instructing him to invite people of low standing, people who had no means to reciprocate. It sounds like the level of pride ran pretty high at this dinner, doesn't it? The guests sought honor and the host wanted accolades.

Paul admonished, "Do nothing out of selfish ambition or vain conceit, but in humility consider others better than yourselves" (Philippians 2:3). Imagine a world where we actually put this into practice. Where we let other people receive the credit. Where someone else is recognized and we're not. Where we give up our seat in the front so another person can be noticed. Where our motive is to bless others and expect nothing in return. Where we willingly assume the lowest position so someone else can be at the top.

In *our* world, we tend to scramble for promotions, recognition and notoriety. But in *God's* world, we don't have to seek promotions. We just need to seek him. Peter said, "God opposes the proud but gives grace to the humble. Humble yourselves, therefore, under God's mighty hand, that he may lift you up in due time" (1 Peter 5:6).

The lower we go, the higher he takes us. And when God lifts us up, we are always within his arm's reach. That's the safest way to the top, isn't it?

Prayer

Jesus, all too often my pride gets in the way and pushes me to pursue acclaims. Please help me have patience to wait for you to lift me up. And if I never rise to the place where I hope to be, make me content wherever you keep me. Amen

WHO'S COUNTING?

 "Lord, how many times shall I forgive my brother?"
Matthew 18:21

I exited our local Kroger store and quickened my pace past the Salvation Army bell-ringer. *"I already gave,"* I called over my shoulder as I hurried to my car. She responded, *"Thank you. God knows the truth."*

Every Christmas season I face the same dilemma: How many times am I obligated to drop money in the Salvation Army bucket? Each time I shop at the store? What about the bell-ringers at other stores? Will I be considered cheap or unconcerned if I don't give money every time at every location? Am I obligated to explain that I already gave? It's quite a conundrum—especially when they remind me that *"God knows the truth."*

He knows the truth that I ALWAYS donate something to bell ringers at least once during the season. A few times I've even bought them hot coffee on freezing cold days. But those times when I'm in a hurry or don't have extra cash, I feel guilty for not giving. Is anybody counting how many times we give?

It's similar to the story in Matthew 18 when Peter asked Jesus how many times he should forgive someone who sins against him. Peter knew that Jewish tradition permitted a person to forgive up to three times. So in a moment of generosity, Peter blurted out, *"Up to seven times?"* He was offering more than double the Jewish tradition. Jesus patiently replied, *"Seventy times seven."* In other words—don't count. Make mercy a generous way of life, not a limiting tradition.

The Psalmist captured the true essence of limitless mercy in Psalm 136 when he repeated this phrase in every verse: *"His mercy endures forever."* The same words are reiterated twenty-six times!

When I was a teenager, our youth group visited a nursing home, and the youth leader asked me to read aloud Psalm 136 to the residents gathered in the dining room. By the time I reached the third verse, I had recited *"His mercy endures forever"* three times. The youth leader stepped over and whispered in my ear, *"It's o.k. if you skip that phrase. It's becoming a little monotonous. Just read it one time at the very end."* Looking back I realize I had skipped what could be the four most important words in the Bible. His mercy is not monotonous—it's limitless.

Now that I think about it, the Salvation Army bell can serve as a gentle reminder that even though the chances to show benevolence may be limited, the opportunities to extend mercy are limitless. Who's counting? God obviously isn't.

Prayer
Lord, thank you for your limitless mercy that flows generously in my direction every day. Teach me to be as generous with forgiveness and mercy as I am with monetary gifts, and help me to lose count. Amen

TRUSTING IN NAME ONLY

 "Trust in the Lord with all your heart and lean not on your own understanding. In all your ways acknowledge him and he will make your paths straight" Proverbs 3:5-6

Serving in a leadership position can create some challenging situations. When I had to confront a couple of younger leaders about a serious wrong-doing on their part, it taught me a lesson that has changed my perception about God.

After praying diligently for wisdom, I set up a time to meet with them. Everything went well—for about five minutes. First, they were receptive. Then they became defensive. By the time we concluded the meeting (early) they were both extremely defiant. If only they had listened, they could have learned some important lessons that would have helped them become much better leaders. Instead, they turned the tables and went on an all-out attack on me and my character.

My initial reaction was to become defensive. I had done nothing wrong, and I needed to speak up and save myself from verbal destruction. So, I prayed for wisdom to defend myself from people who were spreading untruths about me. My conversation with the Lord went something like this:

> Me: *Lord, you know I'm innocent. All I wanted to do was help these kids learn from their wrong-doing. Now you see what they're doing to me.*
>
> God: *I saw it all. What do you want me to do for you?*
>
> Me: *You're my defender. Please come to my defense.*
>
> God: *You call me your defender. But, will you trust me enough to let me do the work of a defender?*

At that moment I realized I trusted God in name only. I called him by name (defender, healer, deliverer, strength). But when it came to fully trusting that he would actually perform those actions for me, I was sorely lacking in faith. I told the Lord that, yes, I would trust him to do the work of a defender. I needed his help and would do whatever he asked.

His first action: He put me under a "gag order," advising me not to speak to anyone of the situation. "Just let me work on your behalf," he said. "If you don't interfere, I'll take care of the situation quickly with the least amount of collateral damage." Gag order? Why me? I was innocent.

As difficult as it was, I maintained my silence and let God work. To my amazement the entire situation was resolved within a few short weeks. If I had taken things into my own hands, the results would have been disastrous.

I learned two things about God. First, he is as concerned about my *response* to difficulties as he is unfairness. Second, if I trust him "in name only" I will miss the opportunity to experience him in action.

Trust me, just watching Almighty God work on your behalf is worth it all.

Prayer

Lord, when I am treated unjustly, help me to be silent so you can speak on my behalf. Slow me down so I can see you work. Then teach me something about your character so my relationship with you is deepened. Amen

THE GRACE TO EMBRACE

 "Before I was afflicted, I went astray, but now I obey your word. It was good for me to be afflicted so that I might learn your decrees. I know, O Lord, that your laws are righteous, and in faithfulness you have afflicted me. May your unfailing love be my comfort."
Psalm 119:67, 71, 75, 76

A friend of mine has suffered from rheumatoid arthritis for years. While her body is in constant pain, her attitude is always cheerful. One day I asked what her secret was for staying so upbeat.

"Arthritis has become my friend," she explained, "because my pain has drawn me closer to the Lord. In the morning my physical discomfort serves as an alarm clock and reminds me to get up and spend time with the Lord. Every day he speaks to me and encourages my heart. If I was pain-free and depended on an alarm clock, I would probably hit the snooze button and sleep in. I would rather be physically weak and spiritually strong than be in the best physical health and suffer spiritual lack."

It's a given that we will experience trials and tribulations. The Bible makes that quite clear. However, for some reason we cross sickness off the list of "God-approved maladies." Why? For one thing, we dislike the physical discomforts that come with being sick. Or we blame ourselves for lack of faith to believe for healing. Sometimes we carry unnecessary guilt, thinking God is punishing us for something we may have done—we're just not sure what we did to gain his disfavor.

Add blame, guilt and frustration to our physical difficulties and it becomes quite a heavy load to carry, doesn't it?

Several years ago I stumbled across a book about healing. It was a very small book and the author shared his simple but encouraging insights about sickness and healing. Early in his walk with the Lord he discovered that with every difficulty came a lesson. So whenever he became ill, he would merely pray, "God, if you're trying to teach me something through my sickness, make me a quick learner. Then heal me. And if you choose not to heal me, show me how you will receive glory through this trial and I will embrace it—for your glory."

Our attitude in a trial makes all the difference. Solomon said, "A man's spirit (some translations say 'attitude') sustains him in sickness, but a crushed spirit who can bear?" (Proverbs 18:14)

When you face an affliction, don't resist it. Instead ask God to reveal something new to you. Your attitude will sustain you and his unfailing love will be your comfort.

Prayer
Jesus, sometimes my afflictions seem like more than I can bear. Please check my attitude so I don't go astray. When I feel crushed beneath the load, help me rise above it all. Give me the grace to embrace difficulties so I can experience your comforting love. Amen

TAPIOCA WORSHIP

 "For you were once darkness, but now you are light in the Lord. Live as children of light (for the fruit of the light consists in all goodness, righteousness and truth) and find out what pleases the Lord." Ephesians 5:9-10

My mother used to say that the way to a man's heart is through his stomach. So when my husband and I first began dating, I would do my best to fix him special homemade desserts—apple pie, cherry pie, brownies—anything I thought would impress him with my cooking. He certainly seemed impressed because he always asked for seconds and took the leftovers home.

One day I was extremely busy and only had time to throw together some instant chocolate pudding. He ate it silently. "Uh-oh," I thought to myself. "I may have just ruined our relationship. I should have taken more time to bake something special."

After we were married I asked him of all the desserts I had fixed for him, which one he liked the best. "Oh, that's easy," he smiled. "The chocolate pudding! It's one of my favorites. My second favorite is tapioca." So that evening I cooked what he wanted—tapioca. Not the basic recipe, mind you. I fixed the special "fluffy tapioca" recipe. It took more time but it looked and tasted amazing. Later as we ate dinner together I watched as he took a bite. "You fixed the fluffy tapioca recipe, didn't you?" he asked. "Yes," I responded proudly.

"Mary," he said "all I wanted was the basic." The basic? But I had worked so hard!

The truth was that I had made something I enjoyed preparing and eating, but it wasn't *his* preference. Fixing dessert had become more about me and what I enjoyed and less about him and what he enjoyed. Yet I hoped he would be impressed with my efforts. I soon learned it didn't take much to please my husband.

Paul instructed us to "find out what pleases the Lord." How do we find that out? We learn what he wants us to do and then we respond with obedience. Jesus admonished his disciples, "If you love me, you will obey what I command" (John 14:15). Genuine love always puts the other person first.

We don't have to try to impress God with our spiritual works baked in a homemade pie crust. He won't be moved by our "fluffy tapioca worship." He's not that hard to please. All he wants is basic, uncomplicated love shown through our obedience. And, if our heart is in the right place, worship can be as easy as pie.

Prayer

Dear Lord, forgive me for finding more joy in my worship than you do. Teach me what brings you pleasure so my devotion becomes simple, pure, and holy. When I over-complicate my acts of worship, remind me that it's all about you. It's not about me. Amen.

WILLING ALIGNMENT

"[Jesus] fell with his face to the ground and prayed, 'My Father, if it is possible, may this cup be taken from me. Yet not as I will, but as you will.' He went away a second time and prayed, 'My Father, if it is not possible for this cup to be taken away unless I drink it, may your will be done.'" Matthew 26:39, 42

Within one week two different people told me, "I really love God but I'm afraid to completely surrender to him because of what he might ask me to do." One situation pertained to healing a relationship. The other dealt with a decision about future ministry. I asked one of the individuals if he thought his might be a situation like Abraham and Isaac—climb the dreaded mountain so God could test his level of obedience. He began to cry. "That's exactly what it is. And I'm conflicted because I don't *want* to be willing. But I do want to be obedient."

I don't think my friend realized the significance of what he was saying. During the time of Isaiah the prophet, God actually told the Israelites if they were both *willing and obedient*, they would eat "the best from the land" (Isaiah 1:19). It's one thing to do what God wants (obedience). It's quite another to *want to do* what God wants (willing). Being obedient merely involves action. Being willing means surrender. Once we relinquish our will, we may lose control but we will gain God's best.

Some people think surrendering to God's will leads to a life of misery and unhappiness. In actuality the happiest people are those who fulfill the purpose for which they were created because their wills are aligned with God's. Total alignment is the safest way to travel.

Mechanics cite four ways to tell if the wheels on a car are out of alignment:

- The vehicle pulls to the left or right
- There is uneven or rapid tire wear
- The steering wheel is crooked when driving straight
- The tires squeal

When our will is out of alignment with God's, we tend to wander off the straight path; we wear out faster; we have to fight harder to stay in our lane—and we squeal a lot in the process. But when our attitude imitates Christ's, we won't just be obedient. We will be willing.

How willing are you to be willing?

Prayer

Jesus, I want the same attitude that you had—not just an obedient heart, but a willing spirit. Make the proper adjustments in my life so my decisions, my attitude, my walk and my talk are in alignment with you. Amen

BE THE CAST

 *"Brothers, if someone is caught in a sin, you who are spiritual should **restore** him gently. But watch yourself, or you also may he tempted. Carry each other's burdens and in this way you will fulfill the law of Christ."*
Galatians 6:1

The crime my twenty-five-year-old relative committed was horrendous. Even so, the long prison sentence he received knocked the wind out of our sails. Yes, he deserved incarceration. Yet, his sentence affected our entire family for the next seventeen years. We were chained to prison rules whenever we visited him.

After the judge pronounced sentence, we watched him being led away in handcuffs. He turned around and took one last look at the family members sitting in the courtroom. It was a heart-wrenching moment for all of us. Then he was gone.

The attorney took us aside and tried to comfort and encourage us. "Whatever you do," he advised, "don't forget about him. Too many people are sentenced to prison and life goes on for the family, but the prisoner is soon forgotten. Do everything you can to stay connected with him because he's going to need all of you when he's released."

Released? Seventeen years is a long time. Could we last that long? Could *he* last that long? We had a decision to make. We could get on with our lives and let him endure seventeen years behind bars, or we could open our hearts and help restore him. He was a broken, repentant man. Who were we to hold the crime against him when God forgave?

The Greek meaning for the word *restore* means to "attach yourself to"—similar to how a cast would be applied to a broken bone. The cast holds the broken bone in place until it can fully heal and become useful again. The cast also serves as an external shield that protects from further injury. If Jesus is the Great Physician, then we become the cast he uses to heal the brokenness in others. When someone is "caught in a sin," our role is to come alongside and help the person stay in place until he is fully healed and restored.

Restoration is hard work. In fact, it's probably harder to help restore someone than it is to be restored. Why would God ask us to do something that is so difficult? Two reasons: First, he is a God of reconciliation and knows the importance of healthy relationships. Second, it is a way to keep us from becoming self-absorbed as we help carry someone else's burden (see Galatians 6:2).

Restoration may be hard, but the end results are well worth the effort. For seventeen years, a small handful of relatives remained faithful in writing letters, ordering books, accepting collect phone calls and visiting regularly. During his incarceration, he earned his bachelor's degree in Biblical Counseling and became trained in a skill that would become a successful career. Around a year prior to his release, he engaged a coach to help him prepare for reentry into society, and he found people who would serve as his accountability partners. A few people played different restoration roles and helped a broken man heal.

Now, three years after his release, he is successfully self-employed, happily married with two step-children and active in his home church. A few times he has even been the "cast" to help another brother who has been caught in a sin.

Whether you need restoration or you play a part in someone else's restoration, remember you can "Cast your cares on the Lord and he will sustain you; he will never let the righteous fall" (Psalm 55:22). When there is true repentance, God becomes less concerned about the sin and more concerned about the cast.

Prayer

Lord, sometimes I am broken and in need of restoration. Please make me willing to allow someone to get close enough to hold me in place until I am fully healed. And, when I am strong enough, give me opportunities to be the "cast" for others who need restoration. Amen

A WIFE OF WORTH

 "A wife of noble character who can find? She is worth far more than rubies. Her husband has full confidence in her and lacks nothing of value." Proverbs 31:10-11

My parents are of Middle Eastern descent. Several years ago while they were on a tour of Palestine, an Arab offered my father twenty camels for my mother. Everyone in the tour group laughed, but I suspect there may have been a few wives who wondered how many camels they would be worth. And why didn't the Arab make an offer to *their* husbands? The proposal of camels was quite a compliment to both of my parents. It validated my mother's worth, and it confirmed that my father had made a good choice in selecting a wife. The reality was that my father didn't choose his wife. His father chose for him. It was an arranged marriage that lasted sixty-nine years.

It's interesting that Solomon would ask "A wife of noble character who can find?" Perhaps he wondered about the rarity even with 700 wives of royal birth (1 Kings 11:3). No doubt most of those marriages were arranged for political advantage rather than for love. It was, and in some cultures today still is, the accepted custom.

In arranged marriages, it's not unusual for love to be low on the list of reasons to get married. In fact, couples often fall in love with each other long after they've said their marriage vows. This is one reason Paul exhorts husbands to love their wives (see Ephesians 5:25, 28; Colossians 3:19). They weren't just to love. They were to follow the example of Christ who loved the church and "gave himself for it." If the husband follows Paul's instructions to show selfless affection to his wife, God will enable him to lavish such love on his bride that she will find him irresistible and respond in love back to him.

The Lord is the initiator of love, and we are created to be responders. "We love because he first loved us" (1 John 4:19). When God the Father sent Jesus into the world, he arranged a marriage between his Son and the Bride of Christ. No hidden agenda. No political purpose. He simply gave what he valued most to those he loved the most.

The day will come when Jesus will present his Bride as a "radiant church, without stain or wrinkle or any other blemish, but holy and blameless" (Ephesians 5:26-27). At that moment, the Son may declare to his Father, "Look what I found. A Bride of noble character. She is worth far more than rubies." No doubt the Father will respond, "Well done."

All the camels in the world can't match that valuation.

Prayer

Oh, Father, thank you for the arrangement you made between me and your Son. I have never felt more valuable than I do right now. I purpose to live my life without spot or blemish and to walk worthy as a part of the Bride of Christ. Thank you for loving me first so I can love you in return. Amen

THE TSUNAMI THAT NEVER HAPPENED

 "But seek first his kingdom and his righteousness, and all these things will be given to you as well. Therefore do not worry about tomorrow, for tomorrow will worry about itself. Each day has enough trouble of its own." Matthew 6:33-34

A few years ago, an earthquake hit an area of the United States and meteorologists warned that the effects would cause a major tsunami around the Hawaiian Islands. My husband and I sat glued to the television to watch news in the making. We were supposed to leave for a meeting, but neither one of us could stop staring at the television lest we missed the tsunami as it happened.

News reporters swarmed the Hawaiian beach while television cameras zoomed in on people swimming and sunning themselves as if they didn't have a care in the world. The sky was blue and the water was calm. We were thousands of miles away, but we yelled at the television in a feeble attempt to warn the people to run for cover. "Can you believe this?" I said to my husband. "Doom is headed their way and they just don't care. What's the matter with those people?"

The longer we waited for the predicted tsunami, the more it became obvious that the meteorologists had missed the mark. Turning off the television, we laughed about the forecast misnomer, trying to hide our own embarrassment for getting caught up in the hype. We almost missed an important meeting over something that never transpired.

Have you noticed how worrying about something is worse than the actual occurrence? The more information we have available to us, the greater our concerns. Like the woman who used the internet to diagnose her physical symptoms. By the time her search ended, she was convinced she would be dead within a year. Frantic, she went to her doctor who was able to convince her that she had misdiagnosed herself, her symptoms were not fatal and she could enjoy life for a long time.

Jesus didn't hide the fact that each day would have some degree of "trouble"—some days more than others. However, he cautioned us to deal with our concerns within a twenty-four hour timeframe. When we borrow tomorrow's troubles, too often the payback is extreme anxiety. That's a hefty price for nothing but trouble. The reality is that much of what we worry about never even happens.

What uncertainties do you allow to capture your attention for which you carry unnecessary angst? Instead of seeking tomorrow's troubles, seek his kingdom. The Prince of Peace guarantees to those under his rule ". . . peace which transcends all understanding [and it will] guard your hearts and your minds in Christ Jesus" (Philippians 4:7). It can't get better than that, can it?

Prayer

Jesus, I acknowledge that you are the Prince of Peace. Help me be a kingdom-seeker and not a tomorrow-borrower. Today please show me how to keep in proper perspective any challenges that come my way. And when I fall asleep tonight, put to sleep any worries from today that don't need to be awakened tomorrow. Amen

MAKING SCENTS

 "But thanks be to God, who always leads us in triumphal procession in Christ and through us spreads everywhere the fragrance of the knowledge of him." 2 Corinthians 2:14

Several years ago, someone gave me a beautiful bottle of perfume. I wanted to savor it, so I kept the lid tightly closed and, ignoring its contents, put the beautiful bottle on display. Recently, I opened the container for the first time and inhaled deeply. Whatever attractive fragrance there was years ago had turned into an offensive odor. I pitched the entire thing—bottle and all—because the fragrance was old and useless.

Later I learned that unused perfume can actually change its scent. What good is possessing a lovely fragrance if it's not put to use?

Life will often lead us to places and situations that are less than fragrant. In those moments we might respond, "This really stinks!" God replies, "Yes, it does. Now take the lid off your Christianity and make it smell good."

Who signed up to be an air freshener? I suppose we all did, because as followers of God, he spreads the fragrance of Christ through us. It's a high call, isn't it? But, sometimes it can lead us right into stinky situations.

Pastor Saeed Abedini has been held in an Iranian prison since 2012, mainly because of his conversion from Islam to Christianity. In spite of his extremely difficult circumstances, he is leading prisoners and guards to the Lord. No matter where he is transferred, he doesn't hesitate to share the "fragrance of the knowledge of Christ." In a Christmas letter to his family and other believers, Pastor Saeed stated, *"We, like Him, should come out of our safe zone in order to proclaim the Word of life and salvation . . . We should be able to enter into the pain of the cold, dark world. Then we are able to give the fiery love of Christ to the cold wintery manger of those who are spiritually dead."* [2]

Maybe God said, "Saeed. I'm going to lead you (in triumphant procession) into a stinky, smelly Iranian prison; and through you I will spread the fragrance of the knowledge of Christ."

What if Saeed chose to keep a lid on his Christianity, bitterly enduring prison without saying a word about Christ? The fragrance would change—or at the very least, it would be unnoticed. On his release he could emerge embittered, demanding justice, rather than a humble, submissive man who spread the fragrance of Christ where the odor of death prevailed.

What does your current situation smell like? Take the lid off your Christianity and let the sweet aroma of Jesus Christ

[2] Sekulow, J. (January 2015). American Pastor Saeed Writes Heartbreaking Christmas Letter from "Hard, Cold" Prison. *ACLJ: Persecuted Church*. Retrieved from http://aclj.org/persecuted-church/american-pastor-saeed-writes-heartwarm ing-christmas-letter-from-hard-cold-prison.

permeate the air. You might be surprised how many people are attracted by the fragrance. Remember, with God in the lead, the results will be triumphant.

Prayer
Father, thank you for letting me be part of your procession of truth. Help me today to carry the sweet fragrance of your Son wherever I go. When I exit the store, or work, or home, let me leave behind an aroma of truth, life and hope for others to inhale. Help me represent you well everywhere I go to everyone I meet. Amen

PROTECTIVE BORDERS

 "Who shut up the sea behind doors when it burst forth from the womb, when I made the clouds its garment and wrapped it in thick darkness, when I fixed limits for it and set its doors and bars in place, when I said, 'This far you may come and no farther; here is where your proud waves halt.'" Job 38:8-11

The sermon was about healing and the pastor invited people who were sick and wanted prayer to come forward. I watched as one woman who had recently been diagnosed with cancer stepped out of her seat and began weeping. The prognosis was not good and she needed a miracle.

As I watched her approach the front of the church, God spoke to my heart, "If I can establish limits on the ocean, how difficult is it for me to put limits on the growth of cancer cells?"

The week before I had been reading the book of Job. As I read Job 38:11, I tried to envision how the "proud waves" knew to obey God. Did he place an invisible sign on the beach—"Halt here!"? Did he simply speak to the waters while his silent echoing words still hover over the watery expanse? It really didn't matter *how* he did it. The important thing is that God is powerful enough to do anything. If he can control the flow of the oceans without batting an eye, how difficult is it to stop a cancerous cell?

God has a way of putting things in perspective, doesn't he? While Job's comforters spent days dialoging about the possible causes of Job's suffering, the Lord patiently listened. As the so-called friends pontificated, Job defended himself. Finally God interrupted with an amazing monologue about his power. Job and his comforters were stunned to silence.

The psalmist reiterated God's power in Psalm 107:20: "He sent forth his word and healed them." The pieces started to fit in my mind. God is powerful enough to speak a simple word and it's done.

As the healing line grew, the Lord prompted me to go to the woman with cancer and speak a word of hope to her. I pulled her aside and whispered in her ear what the Lord had just shown me. She began to weep as we prayed together.

You've probably already figured out the end of the story. Within a week, her doctor confirmed she was cancer free!

When God puts things in perspective, we become a tiny speck in comparison to his greatness. Yet he still uses us if we will step out in obedience and watch him work. How much easier can it get?

Prayer
Oh, Lord, I truly want to be used as your vessel. Please give me ears to hear your words of inspiration, give me faith to speak on your behalf, and give me courage to obey your promptings so others will know your power and glorify your name. Amen

LITTLE THINGS

 "Four things on earth are small, yet they are extremely wise: Ants are creatures of little strength, yet they store up their food in the summer; coneys are creatures of little power, yet they make their home in the crags; locusts have no king, yet they advance together in ranks; a lizard can be caught with the hand, yet it is found in kings' palaces." Proverbs 30:24-28

In the 1800's, Islamists began to invade the African continent, moving north to south. When they reached the middle of the continent, the invasion came to a halt when they encountered a marshy grassland infested with hordes of the deadly tsetse fly. Today, those countries in the African Middle Belt are still divided with the southern parts protected from Islamic influence—thanks to that tiny insect.

Imagine something as minute as a fly having the influence to stop Islam dead in its tracks. God does have a sense of humor, doesn't he?

In today's scripture we read how Solomon noted four creatures that were small in size but large in wisdom. What can we learn from them?

- *Carry our own weight* - Ants can lift fifty times their own weight, and during the summer months they use that strength to store up food for the winter. Carrying our own weight sounds simple compared to what ants contend with. Paul the Apostle said everyone should at least "carry his own load" (Galatians 6:5), and we should take advantage of every opportunity. God will multiply our efforts beyond what we can ask or imagine (see Ephesians 3:20).
- *We need to learn to live with difficulties* – Coneys are timid creatures that live around steep, rugged masses of rock with projections, making it difficult to climb. No doubt their living circumstances contribute to their sense of balance and the strength of their limbs. Our response to challenging situations will either strengthen or weaken our faith. Perhaps we need to become more balanced like the coneys and willingly climb life's crags (see Romans 5:3-5).
- *We need each other* - Locusts have a way of recognizing and honoring the position of their team members. Locusts don't compete. They unify. Solomon said, "Though one may be overpowered, two can defend themselves. A cord of three strands is not quickly broken" (Ecclesiastes 4:12). Let's embrace the person next to us.
- *God can advance our status* – How does the lizard end up in the king's palace? He just does what comes naturally. God can take the most unsuspecting person and place him where he never thought he would deserve to be— supernaturally (see Luke 14:10-11).

Do you feel insignificant? Then you're in the best place for God to show his strength: "My power is made perfect in weakness" (2 Corinthians 12:9).

Prayer

Lord, you are the Creator of all things, and I thank you for creating me the way I am. When I become weary in well-doing, give me the perseverance of the ant. When I lose my balance, strengthen my feeble limbs. When I'm tempted to detach and go it alone, remind me of the progress of the unified locusts. And when I seek notoriety for myself, hold me back until you open the door—supernaturally. Amen

KEEPING PACE WITH GOD

 "I heard the voice of the Lord saying, 'Whom shall I send? And who will go for us?' And I said, 'Here am I. Send me!'" Isaiah 6:8

In relay races, the passing of the baton must be precisely timed. Runners have a certain space in which the baton is handed off and timing is crucial. When the receiver sees the first runner headed toward him, he begins to run, holding out his hand ready to receive the stick. By the time the first runner reaches the receiver, they're running at the same pace and the hand-off is complete.

Some relay trainers instruct the receivers to reach their running pace and not even turn around. "Keep your face forward," they instruct, "and your arm stretched out behind you, hand open, ready to receive. Trust the first runner to catch up with you to pass the baton." It's all about timing and trust.

Moses passed the baton of leadership to Joshua, his young protégé. Joshua was "filled with the Spirit of wisdom because Moses had laid his hands on him" (Deuteronomy 34:9). The poor guy apparently had misgivings about his new role, since

God told him three times to "be strong and very courageous" (Joshua 1:6, 7, 9). The Lord even charged him to not be terrified or discouraged. Joshua accepted the baton and led the Israelites into the long-awaited Promised Land.

Isaiah was a young prophet when he heard God's call, "Whom shall I send?" The Lord had a mission and he needed a receiver. Isaiah was inexperienced but he was ready and willing to receive because he was keeping pace with God. By the end of his life Isaiah served as an advisor to four kings and became a great encourager of Israel.

Jesus made a "hand-off" to his followers when he said, "Go and make disciples of all nations . . ." (Matthew 28:19). The apostles were not perfect, by any means. But Jesus trusted them enough to send them out as church planters and missionaries. The disciples kept pace with the Spirit and the gospel spread throughout the world.

We don't have to wait until we're ready. We just need to be willing. If God trusts us with an assignment, we can be assured he will help us complete it. Remember—it's all about timing and trust.

Are you ready for your assignment? Keep your hand out so you can receive and run.

Prayer
Lord, I want to be a receiver when you are ready to pass the baton of responsibility. Please give me the willingness of Isaiah, the boldness of the disciples and the courage of Joshua. Help me not to release what you put in my hands until the mission is completed. And help me to trust you as much as you trust me. Amen

THE POWER OF THE WORD

 "The unfolding of your word gives light; it gives understanding to the simple." Psalm 119:130

A few years ago I sang in a concert choir that performed in large theaters and concert halls. For one of our acts, concert members dressed in formal attire. The men wore black tuxes and the women wore beautiful black and gold gowns that shimmered in the light.

At our first performance, the choir lined up backstage, waiting for our cue to process to the risers. Looking around at the other singers, I noticed several were wearing red. "How did you get a different color gown?" I asked the woman next to me. "My gown isn't a different color," she said, looking at her dress. "It's black like everyone else's." Then she gasped, "Wow! My dress looks red, doesn't it?" The backstage lighting was very deceptive, making one color look like another. The powerful lighting in the auditorium, however, allowed the audience to see the true colors. If theater lighting can have that kind of effect, imagine the power of the light of God's Word.

I know one young man who had been addicted to drugs for years. In a desperate attempt to change his life, he went on a thirty-day fast and spent that time studying the Bible and praying. When he emerged from the end of his month with God, he was completely drug free and his mind had been transformed. Today he is a minister of the gospel.

An elderly man told me that he had to drop out of school as a child and go to work to help support his family. He spent his teenage and early adult years hiding the fact that he could barely read. Shortly after he and his wife became Christians, she wanted to start family devotions with their family. The man refused because he didn't want his children to know about his being almost illiterate. Out of desperation he begged God to help him learn to read better. Every day he would secretly sit with an open Bible and attempt to understand the words. God honored his faith and "unfolded" to him the ability to read and comprehend. The man became a Bible teacher in his church and, when he died, he left behind a library of hundreds of books.

What separates the Bible from all other books? It is "living and active" (Hebrews 4:12), a claim no other book can make. In a dark world with compromised values, it's reassuring to know we can always find security in God's unchanging Word. If he gives us light and understanding, what more do we need?

Prayer
Lord, thank you for the power of your Word. When I am confused by the instability of the world, bring me back to the security of your Word and unfold truth to me. Help me walk in the light of scripture so I am not misled by false pretenses. Amen

CLOSET CHRISTIANS

 "Be wise in the way you act toward outsiders; make the most of every opportunity. Let your conversation be always full of grace, seasoned with salt, so that you may know how to answer everyone." Colossians 4:5-6

The woman's words surprised me. "Thank you for being brave enough to speak openly about your faith," she said. "I am very inspired to do the same thing." I had just taught a workshop at a secular conference and later discovered that among the attendees were several "undercover Christians." Apparently the fact that I was bold enough to speak openly about my faith encouraged this group of people. What they didn't know was that I wasn't always that courageous. At one time I was a closet Christian who hid behind a locked door.

I hid until someone else who had the confidence I desired challenged me with Colossians 4:5-6. This scripture is Paul's call for Christians to come out of their protective bubbles and speak about their faith with confidence and intelligence.

The key to unlocking the closet is realizing that sharing our faith is not about us—it's about others. When we change the focus from "me" to "you," we will gain the confidence to speak out.

Paul tells us how:

1. *"Be wise in the way you act toward outsiders."* Paul is referring to "outsiders" as people who are outside the faith. Notice this isn't about words. It's about actions. If our lives are above reproach, our words will carry credibility.
2. *"Make the most of every opportunity."* God will lead us to divine appointments that he has pre-orchestrated. He never puts us in "cold" situations, but instead warms the hearts of others who are open to hearing the truth. Make the most of those moments.
3. *"Let your conversation be always full of grace, seasoned with salt."* We do not have to hammer the truth into people's hearts. If our words are soft, kind and gracious, the Holy Spirit will help them land on receptive soil. What we say will create thirst in people who will desire more.
4. *"Know how to answer everyone."* We should be knowledgeable enough about scripture to know what we believe and why we believe it. Then we should practice articulating it clearly.

What's keeping you locked in your closet? Peek out and see who needs you. Then boldly step out and take a stand. Your courageous act will be contagious.

Prayer

Jesus, forgive me for hiding my faith. I am willing to step out and take a stand. Lead me to divine appointments and fill my mouth with the words to speak to those who are ready to hear. Build my confidence so I can build your kingdom. Amen

SEEK AND FIND

 "The kingdom of heaven is like a merchant looking for fine pearls. When he found one of great value, he went away and sold everything he had and bought it." Matthew 13:45-46

While visiting Cairo, Egypt many years ago, I decided to buy a ring from a local jeweler. I was young and inexperienced when it came to international purchases; but a shiny ring marked at $75 caught my eye, and it fit my limited budget. "This is a genuine precious stone," the merchant said. I had no reason not to believe him. Hoping to make a sale, he asked, "How much will you give me for the ring?" We haggled over the amount and finally agreed on $45—half the ticketed price, but still costly for someone who didn't have a lot of money.

"Good bargain for you," he smiled. I left the store feeling quite proud of my negotiating skills. Even our tour guide and a jeweler in Jerusalem confirmed my "good bargain."

When I returned to the States, I went to a local jeweler to have the ring sized to fit my finger. "I bought this in Cairo, Egypt," I bragged. He picked up his eye loupe and began to examine the ring. "By the way, what would you say it's worth?" I was hoping for one more confirmation so I could boast about my great Egyptian find.

"Oh, about two cents," he calmly replied.

"Are you sure?" I nervously asked.

"I'm positive. It's just tin and cut glass."

Considerably embarrassed, I took the ring from the jeweler and slipped out of the store. I haven't worn the ring since. Over the years, it has lost its luster. It sits in my jewelry box as a reminder of wasted money in a hasty purchase.

Spiritual speaking, people have a lot of attractive choices—options that appear to have value but in the end leave a person empty and dissatisfied. Jesus, however, is the find of a lifetime where the search ends and spiritual growth begins. We can't haggle over the cost because no one can place a value on the Pearl of Great Price. And since he is the light of the world, he will never lose his luster.

Let's purpose to take Jesus out of our "jewelry box" and show the world spiritual authenticity. It will lead others on a satisfying search they will never regret.

Prayer

Jesus, thank you for leading me to you. Give me opportunities to share with others the value I have found so they can make the same discovery. I want to decrease as you increase so I never eclipse your light. Make me transparent so others can see your brightness shining through my life. Amen

SPIRITUAL WORKOUT

 "O God, you are my God, earnestly I seek you; my soul thirsts for you, my body longs for you, in a dry and weary land where there is no water. You are my help. Your right hand upholds me." Psalms 63:1, 7-8

The **Jack LaLanne** Show was the longest-running television exercise program. Jack presented fitness and exercise advice on television for 34 years. He worked out every day and made it look effortless. During an interview on his ninetieth birthday he confessed, "I hate to exercise. But I love the results." I was stunned. He always appeared to love what he was doing, but he only endured physical discipline because he wanted to enjoy the benefits—a fit physique and a successful television show.

God has convicted me about my attitude toward practicing spiritual disciplines—like daily prayer time, reading the Word and routine fasting. Often I have approached these activities as inconvenient, mundane or laborious. But I endured them because I knew it was the right thing to do; and, like Jack LaLanne, I wanted the benefits. Of course, I would have preferred to have the blessing without the process. That is until a few years ago when the Lord enlightened me.

I was working with a mentor/coach about a project on which I needed advice. "Give me your insight. What should I do?" I asked. She suggested I form a "master mind group"—a team of individuals who could guide, instruct and encourage each other on their individual ventures. The idea intrigued me and I began to ask God who should become part of my master mind group. The Lord responded, "I am your Master and I have a mind. Ask me for my input." His point was well taken.

The next morning I set aside time specifically to meet with God in our newly-formed alliance. I was really eager to hear his contribution regarding my situation. "Give me your insight," I began. "What should I do?" I waited. He spoke. The Lord shared wisdom that I did not receive from my mentor/coach and would not have gleaned from my own hand-picked master mind group. His eager response to my request meant he enjoyed spending time with me.

Since then, God and I meet regularly. His contributions are generous and wise. It never feels like monotonous exercise. And the outcomes are an added bonus. Peace of mind. A slower pace. Low blood pressure. Less stress. Better decisions.

Turn your spiritual disciplines into a relationship with the Master. You'll love the results.

Prayer

Lord, help me to be like the Psalmist who desired you with every part of his being. Slow me down long enough to enjoy your presence and hear your voice. Amen

ABOUT THE AUTHOR

Mary Selzer is an award-winning author, inspirational speaker, Bible teacher and a professional coach who works with executives, leaders and teams. Her passion is to inspire people to love and live by God's Word. Mary and her husband live in St. Clair Shores, Michigan.

You can read Mary's blogs at maryselzer.blogspot.com, like her Facebook page "A Weekly Quest" and follow her on Twitter at Mary Selzer @mkselzer.

LOOK FOR THESE TITLES FROM OTHER HARTLINE AUTHORS

Marilyn Turk's *Lighthouse Devotions:* Lighthouses—inspiring, symbols of hope, refuge, safety, security, and strength. People the world over are drawn to them and what they represent. Every continent has at least one lighthouse guarding its shores, warning mariners of danger and showing them where they are. God's Word does the same for everyone. Yet it not only provides daily guidance but also eternal direction for safety and well-being. It is no surprise, then, that God used the term "light" to represent what He and His Word are to mankind. *Lighthouse Devotions* are stories about real lighthouses and people who lived in them, and how these stories demonstrate biblical principles found in God's Word.

Elsie Brunk's *God in the Silence* is a Christian devotional containing a message from God for each day of the year. It speaks to inner needs in many different situations, including one's concerns about their welfare due to the unsteady economic situation, feelings of anxiety over the unstable world situation, dealing with a personal crisis, or simply desiring a closer relationship with God.

Chaim Bentorah's *Hebrew Word Study: Ancient Hebrew Words Put into a Biblical Context with the Help of the People Who Ride My Bus* is different from other Hebrew word study books as this book takes a specific passage of Scripture and analyzes it with respect to its historical and cultural background. It takes key Hebrew words in this passage of Scripture and drills down to the very heart, soul and core of the Hebrew word and where appropriate traces that word to its Semitic origins. This is then put into a devotional format using the author's experiences from driving a disability bus to help illustrate and put these Scriptures and Hebrew words into a modern context for every day Christian living.

Kathy Ide's *21 Days of Grace* **series:** Don't you find that life lessons are more easily absorbed through stories, even if they are fictional? But when you have your quiet time with the Lord, you want something with a bit more depth ... and a little bit shorter, right? 21 Days of Grace fits that need. Like Jesus' parables, these stories deal with important life issues in a subtle, unpressured manner. And, as Jesus did, the authors follow up with life applications based on the stories, suggesting how the inherent lessons can be applied to the reader's daily life.